The Forsyth Wickes Collection

FORSYTH WICKES *seated in the library,*
Starbord House, Newport, Rhode Island.

The

Forsyth Wickes Collection

by Perry T. Rathbone

Distributed by NEW YORK GRAPHIC SOCIETY, Greenwich, Connecticut

Museum of Fine Arts

Boston

The entire Forsyth Wickes Collection numbers
some 800 items of which a representative
number are illustrated and discussed
in this handbook.

Cover:
Maurice-Quentin de La Tour, France, 1704–1788.
La Dame en rose.
Pastel. 65.2661.

The entrance hall, Starbord House, Newport, Rhode Island.

The salon, Starbord House, Newport, Rhode Island.

Forsyth Wickes

Forsyth Wickes lived a long and active life and was a passionate collector. From an early age, circumstances guided him in the direction of his principal interest, the art of France in the eighteenth century. As a school boy he spent a year in Paris, lived with a French family and learned the language. The experience must have nurtured also a deep sympathy for the country, for a friend and contemporary relates that at the outbreak of the first World War, Forsyth Wickes was a spirited advocate of immediate involvement on the side of the Allies. His partisanship found scope when the United States entered the war, and he was commissioned a Major in the American Expeditionary Force and became a liaison officer with the French Army. He won the Distinguished Service Medal and the Légion d'Honneur.

Forsyth Wickes' affinity with France only deepened when his legal practice required him to spend protracted periods in Europe. It was then, in 1925, that he bought a house in the rue Weber in Paris and began to furnish it with what became the nucleus of his collection.

Mr. Wickes was descended from old American stock, and he was proud of his ancestry, a fact that impressed my mind when, having the privilege of browsing in the well stocked library of his Newport house, I came upon a family genealogy which he had himself painstakingly prepared. His filial pride was further expressed in the row of old family portraits that hung above the sideboard where a king's ransom in English silver and French porcelain was set out. These forebears had dwelt for generations in the Hudson Valley and in New York where Forsyth Wickes was born on October 26th, 1876. Ties were maintained in Newburgh on the Hudson, where his mother's family, the Forsyths, originated. With the exception of the year he spent in Paris, young Forsyth was sent to school in New York and at St. Mark's in Southboro, Massachusetts. In 1898, he graduated from Yale and afterwards attended Columbia Law School where he and a group of students founded the Columbia Law Review, of which he was the first editor.

8   *The salon, Starbord House, Newport, Rhode Island.*

For many years Mr. Wickes practiced law in New York. But it was in the course of legal work with Royal Dutch Petroleum (the parent company of Shell Oil Corporation for which he was a director and general counsel) with offices in Europe, that the opportunity arrived for Forsyth Wickes to develop his strong but still latent gift as a collector. As a boy, his mother had taught him to respect the quality of old silver and to appreciate the properties of fine porcelain and glass. To furnish his new house, it was natural that his taste should turn to the products of the French eighteenth century when the domestic fine arts reached the summit of perfection. This predilection at the same time provided the wherewithall to fashion an environment at once livable and beguiling, an environment that also reflected Forsyth Wickes' lifelong love of French culture.

His new association brought him into contact with connoisseurs and museum men. René Huyghe and Pierre Verlet of the Louvre and Georges Haummont of the Sèvres Museum were his friends. Above all François Boucher, Director of the Carnavalet Museum, whom he had met in the French Army, befriended and guided him. During these formative years, Forsyth Wickes' knowledge and discernment grew apace, stimulated by the company of his scholarly associates and by the joyous but stern experience of making acquisitions. To his much loved and beautifully bound library of French and English classics, he now added the works on the art of the eighteenth century, the monographs and the catalogues of private collections that no serious *amateur* can do without.

In time, his devotion to French culture and history and his generosity to the institutions dedicated to their study won him wide recognition and many distinctions, rare for an American. He was trustee and later President of the Institut Français, a founder and later President and the Board Chairman of the Lycée Français de New York. He was prominent in raising the necessary money in New York to secure at auction for the Municipal Library of Bordeaux the manuscript of Michel de Montaigne's "Livre de Raison;" and he supported the Committee for Restoration of the Library of the University of Caen, and the Fontainebleau

9

School of Music. He was a member of the Société des Amis de Versailles, the Amis du Louvre, the Musée de Sèvres, and a generous donor of works of art to all three museums. He was especially close to the Musée Carnavalet in Paris to which he donated many objects and documents. For thirty years a director of its Société des Amis, he was named Honorary President of the Board of Directors in the last year of his life.

He was promoted to an officer in the Légion d'Honneur in 1938, to Commandeur in 1949, and to Grand Officier in 1963.

In the late 'twenties, Forsyth Wickes acquired another property — the charming sixteenth century Château de Courmoulin at Gaillon in Normandy, where part of his collection was installed. It was here that I had one of my last visits with him.

Forsyth Wickes was an exceptional raconteur. Surely in his declining years he spent his happiest hours surrounded by his trophies and reliving the chase. Everywhere he had scouted for additions to his collection and each detail of every adventure he savored in his memory from the first scent to the ultimate thrill of possession. Though his vision was sadly impaired, so well stored in his mind's eye were all his works of art that he could see them vividly as he talked.

Forsyth Wickes was a *grand amateur*. Taking knowledge for granted, the essential trait of this rare breed of collector is personal taste and conviction. Everything Forsyth Wickes possessed he understood and loved. Sir Kenneth Clark in his introduction to *Great Private Collections* (New York, 1963) wrote, "The collection of a *grand amateur* should not be too big or too systematic; it must look completely at home in its surroundings and must be related even to the food and the wine on the sideboard. It must, above all, be personal, an extension of the character of the collector." Sir Kenneth could have been describing Starbord House, the last residence of Forsyth Wickes at Newport, Rhode Island. For in this domicile — a moderate sized house of stone, built about 1850 — Forsyth Wickes had brought together in a most ingratiating ensemble the some 800 pieces that comprised his collection; the harvest of forty years of activity. The door opened at Starbord House and immediately you were in the shining presence of much loved objects of many kinds —

pastels and sculpture, porcelains and furniture – arranged with grace
and elegance, with an unfailing eye for nuance, color, and compatibility.
You were exhilarated by the atmosphere, intrigued to explore every
room, every shelf and corner. And the rooms at Starbord House – there
were seven that contained the greater part of the collection – had the
charm of being markedly different; each possessed its own distinctive
atmosphere. When Mr. Wickes bought Starbord House in 1945, he
reduced the first floor to a hollow shell and reconstituted the interior to
make as compatible a background as possible for his collection.
Eighteenth century French mantelpieces, damask-paneled walls, an
expanse of antique parquet, a black and white marble pavement in the
hall created not the impression of a "period" house, but provided a
sympathetic domestic setting, ideal in scale and tone for what it was to
contain, effective almost to the vanishing point of suppressing its original Victorian finish.

No collector ever lived more intimately with his treasures than
Forsyth Wickes. He wished to have everything at hand, within reach
(except of his grandchildren!) so that it could be felt, examined for subt-
leties – the line and texture of a drawing, the decor and makers' marks
of porcelains – discussed and shared with those friends and colleagues
who were fortunate enough to savor the hospitality of Starbord House.
No connoisseur was more in the habit of relating his beloved works of
art "even to the food and wine on the sideboard". For not only were the
latter compatible in their distinction; his dining table, noon and night,
was set with the porcelain of Madame Du Barry and the Prince de
Condé, early English wine glasses and silver.

Forsyth Wickes had a firm conviction that works of art made for
daily use and enjoyment should be shown in that context, in that natural
and easy relationship which a domestic setting suggests. Abjuring the
pedantic, he did not sympathize with the museum practice of displaying
objects in categories and strict historic sequence. In a primarily French
room, he would not hesitate to place an English table or pastel, or an
Italian bronze. Herein lay part of the secret of the charm that pervaded
his domain – sensitivity, conviction, the unmistakable personal touch.   11

Jean Antoine Watteau, France, 1684–1721.
Four Studies of a Woman.
Red, black, and white chalk on tan paper. 65.2610.

12

Drawings and Watercolors

No part of the Forsyth Wickes collection was nearer to its owner's heart than the drawings by French eighteenth century artists. These are the most personal of all, and they bring us into closest contact with the artists of the age. For these reasons, as well as for their warm and unpretentious subject matter, the drawings are chiefly responsible for the intimacy of atmosphere that characterized Starbord House and that happily prevails in the reassembly of the collection in the Museum. They number seventy-nine and reflect the breadth of Mr. Wickes' taste, ranging from the aristocratic elegance of two early eighteenth century drawings of young women by Watteau, to Carle Vernet's sporty view of English jockeys at a race meet of nearly a century later. All the great draughtsmen of the era are present: Boucher, Fragonard, Hubert Robert, Saint-Aubin, Moreau le Jeune, David, Prud'hon and Ingres. But Mr. Wickes' connoisseurship responded as well to first rate works by the lesser masters of the age: Gillot, J. B. Mallet, Vien, Adelaide Labille-Guiard, Cochin, and Boilly, among others. They are executed in all the media characteristic of the period: sanguine, black chalk, watercolor, ink, and ink wash. One of Mr. Wickes' collecting criteria was excellence of preservation. The state of all the drawings is well nigh flawless.

The altogether delightful ink drawing, *Mascarade*, by Claude Gillot (1673–1755), the Flemish-born master of Watteau (1684–1721) heralds the age of the rococo. Gillot was a decorative artist as well as a stage designer and scene painter, especially for the *commedia dell'arte*, and in this little *parada* of masked figures, moving to the strains of a quartet half hidden in the trees, the theatrical inspiration is evident as is the relaxed atmosphere that came with the Regency.

Watteau's magnificent drawing, *Four Studies of a Woman*, is one of the glories of the collection. Feminine charm and grace were hallmarks of the new age. With what mastery these irresistible traits are captured by Watteau's red, white, and black chalk line! The soft gaze of the eyes, the full lips and shapely ear, the fluid line of the bodice, the beguiling tilt of the head are committed to paper under the master's perfect command. Even the placement of the heads in this casual study is instinctively artistic.

"The grace of Watteau is grace itself," wrote the brothers Goncourt. "It is that indefinable touch that bestows upon women a charm, a coquetry, a beauty that is beyond mere physical beauty. It is that subtle thing that seems to be the smile of a contour, the soul of a form, the spiritual physiognomy of matter." The words are a perfect characterization of the Wickes drawing.

The study at the upper left is related to figures in two paintings, *L'Assemblée dans un Parc*, in the Berlin Museum (Dahlem) and *La Gamme d'Amour*, in the National Gallery, London. The drawing belonged to Gabriel Huguier (1695–1772) who engraved and published decorative designs drawn by Boucher, Gillot and others and also amassed a choice private collection. In the nineteenth century it was owned by an English collector known as "Miss James" along with some twenty-five other superb Watteau drawings, all of which were shown at the South Kensington Museum in 1878. A number of them are now in the British Museum. The informality of life that came with the Age of Reason created a new taste for drawings as ends in themselves. What had hitherto been studio notes for the artists' response were now deliberately finished, placed in a French mat, framed and hung on the wall. Boucher indulged heavily in this profitable activity. The virtuoso chalk drawing *Young Woman with Two Cherubs* might well have been done for this purpose. The drawing has an interesting history. It belonged to Sir Joshua Reynolds and is stamped with his mark in the lower right corner. On the back of the eighteenth century mount, we find inscribed, "given me by Boucher, J. Reynolds." In 1752 Reynolds visited Boucher in his studio and recorded the event in his twelfth Discourse telling how he found Boucher merrily painting away at his easel but without benefit of a model. He told the astonished Reynolds that when he was young, studying his art, he found models necessary; but he had done without for many years. We may presume this to be the case with the present drawing which Sir Joshua could have brought from the studio as a souvenir.

By the same token we may easily assume that no actual scene inspired *Landscape with Water Mill*. This rustic idyll is a characteristic Boucher invention deriving from Dutch landscape painting of the previous century as practiced by Hobbema and Jacob Ruysdael. Such drawings were among the first to be reproduced in facsimile by an improved process of engraving, the invention of Gilles Demarteau (1722–1776), whereby effects of pencil and chalk were obtained. The wide distribution of contemporary facsimiles furthered the immense popularity of Boucher.

Gabriel de Saint-Aubin (1724–1780) is the author of the entrancing little watercolor, *L'Entretien galant*. Flirtations, indiscretions, infidelities were the repertoire of most of the artists of the French rococo era. Always piquant and often ironic, the subjects are the very essence of the informal side of social life in the eighteenth century. No one was a wittier observer of the scene than Gabriel de Saint-Aubin who shows us here, by a cosy fireside, the inveterate roué and the incurable flirt. An excited lap dog accentuates the absurdity of the encounter. Both this watercolor and another, *Portrait of a Clockmaker*, in gouache, come from the celebrated collection of David-Weill of Paris.

There are six drawings by Jean-Michel Moreau le Jeune (1741–1814) – portraits, hunting scenes and a landscape. None is more unusual, none could be more endearing, than the little pair of ink and wash drawings of the artist's infant daughter, Catherine Françoise, in ruffled cap and nightgown, asleep in bed. With discreet washes and a few deft strokes of the pen, Moreau describes the perfect repose of innocence. The child was born in 1765 and in 1787 married the artist Carle Vernet; their son was Horace Vernet, the painter of military pictures. These drawings belonged to renowned collectors, not least of them, the brothers Edmond and Jules de Goncourt. Later they were in the J. P. Heseltine and the Mortimer L. Schiff collections.

The French landscapist par excellence of the eighteenth century was Hubert Robert (1733–1808). Devoted friend and traveling companion of Fragonard, the two artists spent student years together at the French Academy in Rome and afterwards as guests of the Abbé de Saint-

Non at the Villa d'Este, Tivoli. Robert became a pupil of Giovanni Battista Panini, master of Rome's architectural grandeur, and his art never ceased to bear the impress of that experience. One of a pair of sanguines, the drawing illustrated is annotated by the artist "tempio di Serapis, Pozzuoli." Typical in subject matter — a Roman view — and characteristic in technique — subtle gradations of red chalk to obtain atmospheric effect — the work easily explains the popularity Robert long enjoyed in an age that was preoccupied with the antique and that romanticized Rome.

Europe's obsession with antiquity, stimulated by the new excavations at Pompeii, spelled the doom of the rococo. The change coincided with the years preceding the Revolution and attained a climax under Napoleon. This turnabout in taste is brought home to us in the brilliant and austere portrait drawing of *Madame Mère*, mother of the Emperor. Dressed in the empire style, Napoleon's mother appears here in a study for the vast canvas by Jacques-Louis David (1748–1825) of the Coronation of the first emperor of the French (Louvre). Napoleon saw himself as a Roman emperor and so did that dedicated classicist and "painter to the Revolution," David. Indeed, the realism of Roman portrait art does not outdo the searching observation of the countenance of the woman who gave birth to the great despot. Pride and satisfaction are mingled in the gaze of the huge Corsican eyes and the self-conscious smile. Succinct and direct, the likeness is a little masterpiece. That Madame Mère's face occupies the very center of David's elaborate composition is not surprising.

Like Gericault and Degas after him, Carle Vernet (1758–1836) was inspired by the animal beauty of the horse. The collection contains a splendid large watercolor by the artist, relaxed and casual in mood, *Cavaliers anglais*, a scene of English jockeys and their mounts. Under billowing clouds in a diffused atmospheric light worthy of Robert, Vernet describes in delicate colors the restless movement of men and animals, the tension of the moments preceding a race. In spite of the fact that he shows us sixteen splendid mounts and a similar number of jockeys, hostlers, and gentleman riders, the drawing is a model of clarity.

Intimacy and a mood of relaxation characterize the graceful sanguine drawing, *La Promeneuse*, by Madame Adélaide Labille-Guiard
(1749–1803), the rival in portraiture of Madame Vigée-Lebrun.
Daughter of the shopkeeper who employed Madame Du Barry in her
youth, Madame Labille-Guiard encouraged the royal mistress in her
artistic pursuits.

One of the most ravishing drawings in the Wickes Collection is the
standing girl seen from the back by Pierre-Paul Prud'hon (1758–1823),
which is nothing less than a new vision of the nude. Drawn in charcoal
heightened with white on blue paper, the simplicity of pose, the sculp-
tural projection clearly show Prud'hon's admiration of the neo-classic
marbles of Antonio Canova, the friend he made in Rome. His artistic
inspiration here, however, was Leonardo da Vinci. From the Italian,
Prud'hon derived his mellifluous contours and exquisite soft modeling
in lights, half lights and blacks, the reflective character of his models,
and the dreaming mood that envelops them. No drawing could better
illustrate Prud'hon's rediscovery of the artistic possibilities of the human
body. Long owned by the pupil and close friend of Prud'hon, Charles-
Boulanger de Bois Fremont (1773–1838) to whom the artist left many
drawings and oil sketches, the *Standing Nude* was later in the collection
of Madame Marbeau.

Paintings and Pastels

Generally larger in scale, richer in color, the twenty paintings and ten
pastels embraced by the collection provide a complement to the numer-
ous drawings. As the very large majority of these pictorial works are
French of the eighteenth century, the ensemble contributes to the
atmosphere of grace and elegance, to the spirit of the rococo that abounds
in the rooms from Starbord House reconstituted in the Museum. Yet
departures from the norm appear here and there – unexpected accents
which prove the receptivity and independence of the collector's eye and

which in a subtle way enhance the personal character of the whole collection. Small court portraits in oil on panel of ladies in stiff lace dating from the age of the Valois and Louis XIII are to be found, as well as small pastel portraits by English artists of the eighteenth century. Mr. Wickes also collected a few French portrait miniatures.

The most important of the works is the celebrated *Déjeuner de jambon* by Lancret (1690–1745). This is the detailed study for the large painting made for the *petits appartements* at Versailles and now in the Musée Condé at Chantilly. The rest of the suite of four paintings, one of them the well-known *Déjeuner d'huitres* which is also preserved at Chantilly, was the work of Jean François de Troy (1679–1752). No one painting could better convey the change in deportment, in accepted behavior amongst the aristocracy which came with the reign of Louis XV, than this rowdy *al fresco* meal. Forgotten is the rigid etiquette of the age of the Sun King. In an elegant garden a group of cronies winds up a splendid repast. Wigs are off. A case of wine is reduced to empty bottles; the joint is consumed; the dinnerware lies in pieces among the scavenging dogs; disorder reigns and the stunts begin. To the merriment of all, the damsel in their midst makes the sign of the stag on the head of one of the celebrants. Lancret brings his sense of composition into full play —a triangle of movement, at its apex a wine-pouring guest with one foot on the table. The picnickers' costumes—blue, yellow, green, and pink— provide a foil for the still-life of ham and porcelain on an expanse of white linen. Gaiety had been ordained by the Regent. *Le Déjeuner de jambon* proves that the injunction was indulged to the hilt. In 1764 the painting was in the famous La Live de Tully collection. Later it was owned by the Marquis de Rochefoucauld-Bayers, and in modern times was in the possession of David-Weill.

Two other works by Lancret figure in the collection. One is a small painting of the most celebrated ballerina of the age, La Camargo. She appears in a moment of relaxation, reclining in a garden, yet decked out in the stiff and elaborate *toilette* of the day. The other is an even smaller and more intimate picture on the gallant theme developed by Watteau. The two artists were fellow pupils in the studio of the theatri-

Nicolas Lancret, France, 1690–1745.
Le Déjeuner de jambon.
Oil on canvas, 1735. 65.2649.

Jean Marc Nattier, France, 1685–1766.
Jeune femme au ruban bleu.
Pastel. 65.2664.

cal painter, Claude Gillot, whose involvement with the flirtatious skits of the *commedia dell'arte* under the Regency gave rise to *scenes d'amour* as a popular subject for painting. This little work, *La Serenade*, painted in a quatrefoil oval shows us a group of three all clad in satin, a seated woman with a fan attended by her cavalier and listening to a musician playing a guitar.

The other genre paintings in the Wickes Collection are by Fragonard and Bernard Nicolas Lépicié, son of the engraver of Chardin's pictures. Mother and child is a recurrent theme in Fragonard's (1732–1806) œuvre reflecting his benevolent and tender nature. The present example, a small oval, representing a young mother dandling her child on her lap while the latter plays with the leaves of a huge book, is done with softness and delicacy, with obvious affection. At play behind the mother are two more happy infants and the group represents a *Caritas* of the rococo. The paint in light tones is brushed on in Fragonard's effortless technique, enveloping the subject in a flood of bright atmosphere. The genre works of Lépicié (1735–1784) are charming prose compared with Fragonard's instinctive poetry. Two excellent examples are to be found in the Wickes Collection. Both show Lépicié's derivation from Chardin. *La Cuisinière* depicts the interior of a scullery with the servant and her house cat seated in a rustic chair plucking a goose. The subject is emblematic of the sentimental interest of the age in the humbler levels of society. *Le jeune écolier* is a winning pastel portrait of a sandy-haired boy in a half length with a portfolio tucked under his arm. Like Chardin's likenesses, it avoids the artifice of manner of the standard eighteenth century portrait. Lépicié's biographer, G. P. Dreyfus, presumes that it represents the son of the architect de la Fosse, as the portfolio is so inscribed.

With the exception of a beautiful small painting by Hubert Robert, all the other paintings and pastels in the collection are portraits, mostly of women. The most splendid of all is the beautiful *La Dame en rose* by Maurice Quentin de La Tour (1704–1788), unsurpassed by any work of the artist in America (see cover). Dressed in a glowing pink silk basque and white bodice, adorned with ribbons and lace, perfectly posed

21

and holding a letter, the lady (alas, unidentified) wears an expression of supreme composure. She is the personification of the wealth, privilege, and security, not to mention the taste, the refined manners, the rococo splendor, of the *ancien régime*. In a sense, this portrait is an emblem of the entire Forsyth Wickes collection. For it was for such privileged clients that the craftsmen of the age bent their efforts: the *ébénistes* perfected magnificent furniture; the designers, potters, and painters created exquisite porcelains; the sculptors and founders fashioned bust portraits, gilded *chenets*, candelabra, and mounts for vases and clocks; the carvers and gilders made the frames which in design and execution surpass those of any other culture. The Wickes Collection abounds in these embellishments. Appropriately, de La Tour's *Dame en rose* is surrounded by the most sumptuous frame of all. It is a classic of French taste and workmanship. The unusually broad side and top members, composed of a sequence of straight moldings derived from the classical repertoire, are interrupted at the corners by scrolls, deep and richly carved and mantled with acanthus and laurel leaves.

Quentin de La Tour was a portraitist and pastelist exclusively. While he outshone his contemporaries of the same discipline, he had his competitors, Nattier, Perronneau and Drouais, and the popular lady artist from Venice, Rosalba Carriera. All these are represented in the collection.

Jean Marc Nattier (1685–1766) was the court flatterer who understood the demand for grace, the vogue for artifice. The latter he pushed to a new level by reviving the taste for the glorification of his sitters by posing them as personifications of antique deities. In his less pretentious moments he simply idealized his subjects as embodiments of beauty and grace. Such a work is the lovely pastel of the *Jeune femme au ruban bleu* who ingratiates the viewer with her perfect features, her melting eyes and roseate lips, her utter femininity enhanced by lace at her bodice, a bow at her neck, a nosegay of roses in her hair.

Jean-Baptiste Perronneau (1715–1785) is represented by a soft and vaporous pastel of a lady but also by a surprising subject for a French artist, *The Earl of Huntingdon*, a descendant of the legendary Robin

Hood, as Mr. Wickes liked to point out. And to be sure the lively expression and alert pose recall the character of his forebear. Painted in oil, the portrait dates from 1753, the year it was exhibited at the Salon and the year Perronneau was admitted to the Academy.

The visit to Paris in 1720 and again in 1721 of the popular Venetian pastelist, Rosalba Carriera, is sometimes cited as the principal artistic inspiration of the youthful Quentin de La Tour. However that may be, he could not have failed to take note of her phenomenal success in reviving the art of painting with colored chalks. No better proof of Rosalba's acclaim need be sought than the beguiling likeness of Louis XV himself in the Wickes Collection. This portrait of the boy monarch resulted from one of Rosalba's two visits to Paris. In her diary she records her excursion to Versailles in order to make a study for the king's portrait which was the basis of this pastel and two others. If one forgets the peruke and jabot, the orange moiré coat and Maltese order, the subject does look to be his age at that date – namely ten or eleven years. The vaporous modeling of Rosalba's chalk technique, the soft beauty of her effects swept her to the summit of popularity among the ladies of the court. Her style was not unsuited to the delicate face of the King at this moment between boyhood and youth.

One of the most fashionable of all the portraitists of the rococo age was François Hubert Drouais (1727–1775) who in 1762 painted the likeness of the beautiful *Mademoiselle Hainaut*, one of the mistresses of Louis XV. She later became the Marquise de Montmelas. Fancy dress was a frequent affectation of rich and well placed persons in the eighteenth century. "Cavalier" costumes appear in the portraits of Fragonard especially. Mademoiselle Hainaut seems to have chosen an ensemble reminiscent of the harem – certainly appropriate for a courtesan – for she is dressed à la Turque; or is it à la Polonaise as a compliment to the Queen, Maria Leszczynska? In any case, the costume suited the talent of Drouais who loved to embellish his portraits with detail. Formerly in the collection of the Comte de Tournon at the Château de Montmelas it was later in the Arthur Veil-Picard collection.

The grandeur of architectural space, dramatized by light and accentuated by the presence of diminutive human figures, animated the artistic impulse of Hubert Robert from the time of his student years in Rome to the end of his career. The characteristic Robert is a large decorative composition, somewhat diffuse in composition. The Wickes example has the virtue of being small in scale, concentrated in design. *L'Éscalier des lavandières*, signed and dated 1796, is an exciting invention, an echo of Rome remembered: massive tall buildings, a long flight of steps pierced with dramatic passages of light, a series of receding arches, thrilling perspectives and in the foreground the picturesque activity of the washerwomen.

Porcelains and Faience

Forsyth Wickes was peculiarly susceptible to the charm and beauty, not to say the historical connotations of high ceramic art. Knowledge and sensitivity are unmistakably evident in the great number of porcelains and faiences he brought together over many years. Wide in range, the collection embraces examples from many of the porcelain centers of France, Germany, and England. The French faience factories of Rouen, Sceaux, Niderviller and Marseilles are also represented. The assemblage proves Mr. Wickes' unfailing discrimination, the refinement of his taste, and his insistence on perfect condition. Three hundred and ninety-one pieces comprise the collection, the majority of them of French origin and the preponderance coming from the Royal Manufactory at Sèvres. But scores of masterful pieces from the porcelain factories of Chantilly, Vincennes, Mennecy, and Tournai are to be found. The wares of the celebrated factories of Germany also figure prominently, the greatest number deriving from the Meissen workshops (sixty-six pieces). Multiple examples – table ware, ornamental pieces, and figurines – provide an account of the prodigious activity at Nymphenburg, Hoechst, Frankenthal, Ludwigsburg, Berlin, and Vienna. There are sixty-two pieces of English porcelain; fifteen of them are figurines originating at the famous centers of Chelsea, Bow, and Derby, while the balance are plates, bowls, vases, and tureens, made at Longton Hall and Worcester.

As already noted, Mr. Wickes' collection was formed to be lived with and used. In consequence, porcelain and faience were to be seen throughout the house, on his dining table, on mantelpiece or commode as garniture, or grouped together in cabinets and arrayed on open shelves, providing in every room notes of entrancing color and exquisite detail. Likewise, out of respect for Mr. Wickes' philosophy of display, ceramics are found in all the rooms that house the collection in the Museum. Almost inevitably there are also examples of Chinese porcelain, certain forms of which found favor at the courts of eighteenth century Europe: K'ang Hsi and Ch'ien Lung pieces superbly mounted in French ormolu. Yet the collector's eye on occasion led Mr. Wickes beyond the programmatic search for the wonders of the eighteenth century. For example, his vision beguiled him into acquiring two fine pieces of early Chinese pottery, such as remained unknown until modern times: a large unglazed T'ang dynasty horse and a glazed seated figure of a T'ang court lady.

The scholarly approach to collecting that characterized Mr. Wickes' activity prompted him to buy two unusual examples of the faience of Rouen, made in the seventeenth century under the influence of the prestigious majolica wares of Italy. These bold, brightly colored Italianate pieces are harbingers of the extensive production at Rouen of a type of faience that became thoroughly French in style.

Among the fifteen pieces of French faience are distinguished examples of Sceaux, a factory capable of making porcelain but prevented from doing so until 1775 by the royal rights accorded to the Sèvres factory. By the same token, Sceaux was not permitted to decorate porcelain in color or gold until 1784. Sceaux faience, on the other hand, which has a characteristic creamy glaze, was decorated with gay color from an early date. The ware is represented by a fan-shaped rose-colored vase and stand painted with scenes derived from Boucher, and a pair of small and most delicate faience urns richly decorated with *scenes gallant* in cartouches and surmounted with pierced lids. But most important of all is a soup tureen and platter of charm and authority, showing in its shape the influence of contemporary silver vessels, and decorated with vigorously painted groups of birds and animals. The knob of the lid takes the form of a lemon.

The Wickes collection abounds in the rare and early soft paste porcelains made at Chantilly, Mennecy, Vincennes, and lastly at Sèvres.

Of surpassing delicacy both in color and simple form are the early products of the Chantilly factory. Founded by the Prince de Condé in 1725 and granted a patent ten years later, the principal inspiration of the wares of Chantilly was Japanese shape and ornament, in particular Imari porcelain of the so-called "Kakiemon" type, a large collection of which had been formed by the Prince. But the glaze also has its own special character resulting from the admixture of tin-ashes which produced the beautiful opaque milky whiteness such as that found on tinglazed faience of Delftware. In this respect, Chantilly differs from all other porcelains whose glazes are clear. A cylindrical jar with lid fitted with bronze-gilt rims is descorated in outline style with the familiar encircling dragon, another legendary beast and stylized floral ornament taken from the Japanese repertory. It is complemented by a set of four smaller white toilette jars which follow the same clean cylinder shape much admired by the Oriental potter. A pair of cachepots with flaring scalloped rims bear the same dragon decor. Similarly painted, but purely French in shape, is a singularly beautiful small ewer and basin. Not least of the Chantilly pieces is a flower holder in the form of a seated Chinese figure or *Magot* in pure milk white with mobile head and hand. It was formerly in the collections of the Earl of Coventry and J. P. Morgan.

The famous soft paste porcelain of Vincennes appears in eleven examples – among others two statuettes in white, a pair of cachepots in turquoise with floral adornment, a pair of perfume burners, a ewer, and a celebrated tureen with stand. An offshoot of Chantilly and the parent of Sèvres, the Vincennes factory flourished from an early date under royal patronage. Halting first efforts in 1738 were made firm in 1745 by new capital, the granting of special privileges and the appointment of Jean-Claude Duplessis, the royal goldsmith, in charge of modeling,

Soup tureen and stand.
Sceaux faience, ca. 1770. 65.2026.

Soup tureen and stand from a service ordered by Catharine II of Russia.
Model by Jean-Claude Duplessis. Decorators Dodin and Pierre.
28   *Vincennes porcelain, 1756. 65.1885.*

and later of the famous sculptor, Etienne-Maurice Falconet. Hardly less distinguished were the chemists of Vincennes, Jean Hellot and his assistant and later his successor, Pierre-Joseph Macquet. For it was the scientific endeavors of the factory—after its removal to Sèvres in 1756—that finally led in 1769, to the first manufacture in France of hard paste or true porcelain.

The tureen is Vincennes at its most sumptuous. Modeled in 1756 by Duplessis, its flowing lines and sensuous form are derived from silver models. Topped with a knob in the shape of an orange, ornamented with reserve panels painted with cupids, flowers, and fruit, this royal object is richly gilded and its green glaze has the velvety quality characteristic of Vincennes. The piece comes from the Hermitage and is said to have been made for Catherine the Great. The pair of perfume burners in the form of turquoise snail shells with clustered shells for knobs and spiral shells for feet are of extreme rarity. They were treasured by Horace Walpole at Strawberry Hill.

Sèvres was the most prolific of all the French factories. In the Wickes collection it is the most richly represented. There are some one hundred and twenty-two pieces, the great majority of soft paste. Among the most important is the famous garniture known as the "Coventry Vases," a pair of fan-shaped pieces on porcelain stands which belonged to the Sixth Earl of Coventry and later to J. P. Morgan. They are glazed with rose Pompadour and green, embellished with gold, and painted with scenes in the Flemish manner. These pieces together with another simi-lar garniture of three fan-shaped vases, glazed in blue with scenes paint-ed in 1758 by Dodin (also from the Morgan collection, but formerly belonging to Prince Demidoff at the San Donato Palace, and prior to that to the Earl of Dudley), represent soft paste Sèvres at its most refined and sophisticated and at the height of the craze for porcelain in the 1750's. There are several exquisite *ecuelles* (shallow bowls with lid and saucer) of most graceful shape and delicate color that possess the same ultra-refinement, as well as a remarkable variety of cups and saucers. Throughout the collection, historic significance often comes into focus. For example, there is a set of charming Sèvres soup plates made for

29

Pair of snail-shaped incense burners.
Vincennes porcelain, ormolu mounts, ca. 1755. 65.1859–60.

Pair of jardinières à éventail (flower holders) and stands,
the so-called Coventry Vases.
Sèvres porcelain, 1759. 65.1799–1880.

Ecuelle and tray. Decorator Jean-René Dubois.
"Rose marbré de violet" Sèvres porcelain, 1761. 65.1786.

Pair of vases, mounted as perfume burners, made for Augustus the Strong.
Meissen porcelain, decorated in the Chinese manner
by Loewenfinck, ca. 1728. 65.2095.

Soup tureen with boar's head finial and stand,
painted with Turkish battle and camp scenes after Augsburg prints.
34 Meissen porcelain, ca. 1740–45. 65.2072.

Madame Du Barry bearing her cipher in gold and a garland of roses. Sèvres hard paste porcelain is found in a superb oval dish decorated in the anti-rococo, neo-classical style that came with the accession of Louis XVI (1774) and the growing enthusiasm for antique taste as it was discovered in the new excavations at Pompeii. The dish was part of a service of seven hundred and forty-four pieces made on order of Catherine the Great of Russia for the palace at Tsarskoe Selo and bearing her monogram "E II" for Ekatrina II.

The greatest of all the porcelain factories of Europe was that of Meissen. Under the patronage of Augustus the Strong, King of Saxony, it was not only first of its kind, but also the most prolific, the most inventive. The factory flourished from its founding in 1710.

Historically important because it was the site of the European discovery of the secret of the Orient, the formula for making true, or hard paste, porcelain, Meissen became artistically first rank by virtue of its great modelers and painters — men like J. J. Kaendler and J. G. Herrold — and the pride of its patron King. One might say that the significance of Meissen could also be measured by the stimulation it provided elsewhere. The masterpieces of Sèvres were achieved in competition with the princely products of the Saxon kilns.

Like the first pieces from the Chantilly workshops, early Meissen is often Oriental in inspiration. Among the very finest in the Wickes collection is a pair of hexagonal vases painted in the Chinese manner by Loewenfinck and marked with the monogram of Augustus the Strong. They are mounted as perfume burners in rococo bronze *doré* with a cattail motif on the handles, the lids crowned with dragons. No less beautiful is a pair of hexagonal lidded jars of about 1730 with "Kakiemon" decoration copied from a Japanese example in the royal collection and bearing the early crossed swords mark. Kingly in the richness of its painted and gilded decor and thoroughly European in style is the magnificent tureen and platter surmounted by a boar's head and dating from about 1740–45.

A wide variety of shapes and styles of ornament are to be seen amongst the many Meissen pieces: trays, sugar boxes, bowls, teapots, coffee pots,

Incense burner in the form of Chinese figures astride an elephant.
Celadon Meissen porcelain, ormolu base, ca. 1730.

36   *65.2028.*

and vases. There are fifteen figurines, five of them modeled by Kaendler. Perhaps the most rare is an incense burner which is truly an Oriental idyll: a celadon elephant bearing a dreamy trio, one with a lute, another holding a censer, the third in contemplation. It is mounted on a splendid base in bronze *doré*.

High baroque taste informs the magnificent pair of Nymphenburg porcelain figures of Venus and Aeolus modeled about 1765 by Auliczek and mounted as bronze *doré* candelabra. Several figurines without mounts represent the factories of Frankenthal and Hoechst.

Among the English porcelain, the products of Derby, Chelsea, and Bow are conspicuous in no less than ten figurines. Of these, the most spirited and original of all are the pair of so-called "Derby boys." The guitar player and drinking boy are each seated amidst a burst of white porcelain flowers held on bronze stems. The brilliant white and royal blue of Worcester of the Dr. Wall period — thirty-two-pieces — make a most dramatic display of this famous porcelain. Characteristically English are the softer shapes, the rippling line of the profiles as well as the very delicate painting of the bird, floral, and butterfly decoration. Especially rare are the tureen with its florid handles and finial and the pair of covered vases made at Longton Hall in Staffordshire.

Sculpture

The relatively small scale of the rooms of Starbord House dictated that Forsyth Wickes collect sculpture of modest dimension. All but one of the twelve portrait busts are less than life size, and all of the figurative pieces are suitable for placement on small stands, commodes, or mantelpieces. Among works by some of the most famous sculptors of eighteenth century France, there are also those by lesser masters. As in all other areas of the collection, personal taste was the ultimate criterion.

A fine bust portrait of Louis XV, perhaps after a marble by Jean-Baptiste Lemoyne, was made at the Ludwigsburg faience factory in 1746. A second, full length, colored, portrait of the king, made of Ni-

Venus and Aeolus. Models by Domenico Auliczek.
Nymphenburg porcelain, mounted in ormolu candelabra, ca. 1765.
38   *65.2105–6.*

derviller faience, seems to find its model in the splendidly pompous figure of Augustus Rex fashioned by J. J. Kaendler for the Meissen factory.

One of the most striking of the portraits is the subtle likeness of the Marquis de Bire by Houdon which comes from the David-Weill collection. This marble bust of the Treasurer of the Province of Arras under Louis XVI is signed and dated 1786.

The quiet realism of Houdon finds a worthy precursor in the small terra-cotta posthumous bust of the Archbishop of Cambrai, François de Fenélon dating from 1724, and attributed to Jean-Louis Lemoyne (1665–1755).

There are four enchanting small busts of women. The earliest are in terra-cotta; one of the actress, Mademoiselle Dangeville, by Jean-Baptiste Defernex, signed and dated 1752 (formerly David-Weill collection); the other of Madame Olivier by Augustin Pajou (1730–1809) signed and dated 1774. From the hand of Joseph Chinard (1756–1813) of Lyons, the leading portrait sculptor of the Directory, comes a superb portrait bust of a man as well as the charming bust in plaster of a woman artist, thought to be Madame M. Charpentier.

The svelte lines and classic calm of Etienne-Maurice Falconet's (1716–1791) style are beautifully revealed in two works – a Sèvres soft paste biscuit group of *Pygmaleon and Galatea*, modeled after him, and a marble figure of a *Baigneuse*, after his follower, Christophe Gabriel Allegrain (1710–1795). The former comes from the famous collection of Prince Demidoff at the San Donato Palace, Florence, and prior to that from the Earl of Dudley.

In contrast, the playfulness, the sensuality of the rococo is expressed in the terra-cotta group by Claude Michel called Clodion (1738–1814). *Two Bacchantes Dancing* brilliantly displays the artist's command of movement, his perfect sense of balance, above all his passion for spirited abandon. Signed and dated 1800, the group comes from the Paris collection of Baron Gustave de Rothschild. Hardly less winning is the terra-cotta figure of a *Faunesse with Tambourine* by Clodion's pupil Joseph-Charles Marin (1759–1834).

A charming pair of children, emblems of Reading and Writing, and modeled in biscuit porcelain by a French sculptor as yet unidentified, were repeated by Johann Peter Melchior for the monument to Elector Karl Theodor of the Palatinate, founder and protector of the porcelain factories of Frankenthal and Hoechst.

The independence of Forsyth Wickes' eye is illustrated by the magnificent Florentine bronze of a *Nereid Riding a Sea Monster*. Clearly close to Giovanni da Bologna, this unique cast (coming from the Hainauer collection in Berlin), foreshadows all the curvaceous opulence of form that was developed in the baroque and that led to the rococo taste of the eighteenth century.

Closely related to the sculpture are the decorative pieces in the collection that were the embellishments of all aristocratic salons of the age: andirons, sconces, clocks, and elaborate ormolu mounts for porcelains often imported from the Orient.

Of exceptional brilliance are two pairs of gilt bronze *chenets*. One set, attributed to Lambert-Sigisbert Adam, is composed of wildly curvaceous forms reminiscent of swirling water and surmounted by bearded mermen blowing tritons. The other rarer and somewhat less exuberant set are decorated with amorini and bear the arms of King Stanislaus Leszczynski of Poland, who in 1736 became Duke of Lorraine.

As already noted, a number of Oriental porcelains were transformed into gorgeous princely ornaments by virtue of their ormolu mounts. Perhaps the most splendid is a pair of bright blue Ch'ing dynasty vases in the form of coupled fish adorned with flamboyant mounts that provide a base and handles for them. These extravagant pieces are thought to be the work of the royal goldsmith and modeler, Jean-Claude Duplessis and it has been suggested that they were made for Madame de Pompadour, the fish serving as a reference to her surname, Poisson. Of similar brilliance are the mounts that envelop a deep blue large Ch'ing dynasty vase in the manner of Pierre Germain, formerly in the Marquis de Ganay collection. The crowning ornament takes the forms of a conch shell, oyster shells with pearls and coral twigs. From the collection

Mantel clock. On fluted Sèvres porcelain column, chased bronze-gilt figures of draped nude in the manner of Falconet holding two hearts and a miniature portrait (Marie Antoinette?), cupid and begging dog. Marble base, ormolu mounts, dial inscribed: Ageron, Paris, ca. 1779. 65.2236.

of the Earl of Lansdale, Lowther Castle, come a pair of crackled celadon bowls richly mounted in ormolu so that the sober Chinese vessels become extravagant expressions of rococo taste. Other mounted pieces from Nymphenburg, Meissen, and Vincennes have been touched upon in the discussion of the porcelains.

Related to the practice of combining porcelain with gilded bronze is perhaps the finest of the seven clocks in the Wickes collection. This is a mantel clock on a marble base with a Sèvres porcelain green and white fluted column. Against it leans a draped nude fashioned in gilt bronze and holding in her hand a pair of hearts, symbolizing friendship, grace, and beauty. On the column's top, she steadies an oval portrait perhaps of Marie Antoinette, while her putto companion plays with a lap dog. This extraordinary conceit which is as delicately finished at the back, is fully in the spirit of Falconet. Three other marble and ormolu clocks are designed in a similar Louis XVI style. Contrast is provided by a charming wall clock by Jean Moisy in which the dial is surrounded by rippling rocaille motifs, flowers, and two sporting amorini; and another example of gleaming bronze *doré* for table or *cheminée* in which the clock is held by a reclining woman.

Furniture

France in the eighteenth century produced furniture that has rarely been equaled in the whole history of cabinet making. Intrinsic beauty of form, refinement of finish and adornment, perfection of joinery — these hallmarks of the best the age produced commanded Mr. Wickes' discriminating eye and his immense capacity for appreciation. Moreover the associative factor of former ownership — the celebrated persons for whom much eighteenth century furniture was known to have been made — delighted the collector's romantic imagination. All the forms that flowered throughout the development of that century and that were at the same time suitable to an unpretentious house of moderate size

Pierre Macret, Paris, 1727–96. Lady's writing desk (bureau de dame).
Veneered red, gold, and black lacquer with Chinoiserie decoration, ormolu mounts.
65.2506.

45

appealed to Mr. Wickes as a collector. Yet as in the case of pictures and porcelains, he was not exclusive in his attitude. He could not resist a superb little Hepplewhite console. He wished to have a sideboard; the French did not make sideboards. So he acquired a fine Adam piece from the collection of Lord Walsingham. The focal point of the entrance hall is a magnificent Chinese lacquer cabinet on a richly carved Charles II base which came from the Earls of Chesterfield at Bretby Hall in Derbyshire.

The earliest example of French furniture is a commode of the late Régence period. Probably the work of the cabinetmaker and sculptor Charles Cressent, this stalwart piece with opulent mounts in bronze *doré*, admirably illustrates the transition from the grandiose and pompous style of Louis XIV to the lighter and more rhythmic forms that reach the height of their development in the reign of Louis XV. The restraint of the crisp bronze ornament and the organic logic of the piece underlie its harmony.

The collection is richest in works of the Louis XV style. The major room in the suite is amply furnished with a settee and six matching *fauteuils* made of the curvaceous carved beech frames typical of the period and upholstered in the original Beauvais tapestry made after designs illustrating Fontaine's fables by the foremost artist for the looms, Jean-Baptiste Oudry (1686–1755). The suite was formerly in the collection of Clarence H. Mackay.

A superlative red and gold lacquer *bureau de dame* is conceived almost like a piece of hollow sculpture. Indeed the organic shape of the desk recalls a shell more than any other natural form, and it reminds us of the pervasive influence of shells with which the fantastic *rocailles* were adorned and the fact that sea shells were widely admired and collected at the time. Signed by the ébéniste, Pierre Macret, the bureau is considered his masterpiece.

The little jewel cabinet attributed to Joseph or Bernard van Risen Burgh is exquisite and feminine, and like the bureau, emblematic of the taste of the age of Louis XV, the taste for intimacy, for small rooms, and informality. Lacquer surfaces were rivaled by marquetry. Van Risen

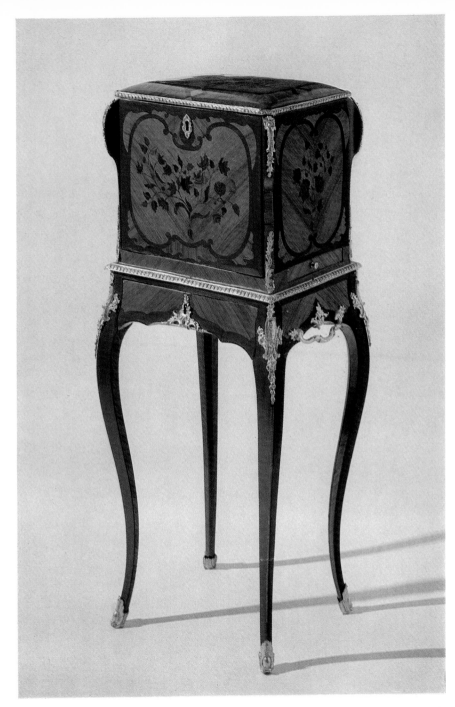

45

Joseph or Bernard van Risen Burgh (attributed). Jewel and writing cabinet (bonheur-du-jour),
Paris, ca. 1750. Veneered kingwood and palisandre wood with marquetry, ormolu mounts.
A gift of Marie Antoinette to Princess Isabelle Lubomirsky. 65.2504.

Burgh designed and executed the surfaces of this jewel case in contrasting woods with consummate taste and craftsmanship. This piece was made at the order of the Queen for her friend the Polish Princess Isabelle Lubomirsky and remained in Lancut in Poland in the collection of Count Potocki until the outbreak of World War II.

The more severe straight-lined style with classical ornament that evolved under Louis XVI is exemplified in exceptional works by two of the greatest cabinetmakers of the time, Georges Jacob and Jean-Henri Riesener. One may see the work of the former in a very fine pair of *voyeuses* or viewing chairs that were made by him for the gaming salon of the King at the royal château at St. Cloud. They are signed and marked with the number of the royal inventory of the Garde Meuble and may therefore be dated 1787. Like English gaming chairs they were built to be sat upon astride, the top rail serving as an arm rest.

The hand of J.-H. Riesener, the greatest ébéniste of the end of the century, is unmistakable in the noble little reading table which is attributed to him. The piece is made of mahogany, and its compact interior hides intricate drawers and a book rest. All the straight lines of the table are enriched and accentuated with gilt bronze ornament derived from the classical repertory which supplanted the sensuous curves of the rococo.

In addition to the Régence piece, there are five large and small commodes in lacquer and marquetry with customary veined marble tops. Perhaps the most beautiful of these is the large marquetry piece with bronze *doré* mounts which comes from the Maurice Wertheim collection. Of particular interest are a pair of black lacquer *encoignures* or corner cupboards in the Louis XV style decorated with large birds and flowers.

*　*　*

No curator would claim that the ideal in presentation had ever been attained within the walls of a museum. Works of art have been created for other, very different, purposes. Museum installation is at best a compromise. But it was Forsyth Wickes' ardent desire that his philosophy underlie the display of his collection in the Boston Museum.

Commode. Veneered black lacquer with Chinoiserie decoration,
ormolu mounts, Paris, ca. 1760. 65.2513.

In consequence, the collection has been placed in a specially constructed suite of rooms corresponding in size and approximating the character and décor of the rooms that Forsyth Wickes created at Starbord House. Some elements have been transferred from Newport, eighteenth century mantelpieces, a parquet floor, and the carved English woodwork of one room. For reasons of circulation and security, certain departures from the plan of the rooms and the placement of objects at Starbord House were inevitable. But these compromises have not seriously impaired the recreation of the delightful atmosphere of their former setting.

49

Claude Gillot, France, 1673–1733. Mascarade. Brown ink. 65.2572.

François Boucher, France, 1703–1770. Young Woman with Two Cherubs.
Sanguine crayon heightened with white on tan paper. 65.2538.

François Boucher, France, 1703–1770. Landscape with Water Mill.
Black, blue, ochre, and red pastel heightened with white on blue paper.
50 *65.2543.*

Gabriel de Saint-Aubin, France, 1724–1780. L'Entretien galant.
Watercolor and gouache. 65.2604.

Jean-Michel Moreau, France, 1741–1814. Petite fille endormie
(the artist's daughter, Catherine Françoise).
52   *Pen and gray wash. 65.2592–93.*

Hubert Robert, France, 1733–1808. The Serapeum, Pozzuoli.
Sanguine crayon. 65.2601.

S.A.J. Madame Mère
de S.M. l'Empereur
par David.

Jacques-Louis David, France, 1748–1825.
Madame Mère (Mother of Napoleon I).
54   Black crayon. 65.2555.

Carle Vernet, France, 1758–1836. Cavaliers anglais.
Pen, black ink, and watercolor. 65.2606.

55

56

Adélaide Labille-Guiard Vincent, France, 1749–1803. La Promeneuse.
Black and white chalk on blue-gray paper which has faded to light brown.
65.2608.

Jean-Baptiste Mallet, France, 1759–1835. La jolie visiteuse.
Gouache on paper. 65.2585.

58

Pierre-Paul Prud'hon, France, 1758–1823. Standing Nude.
Charcoal heightened with white chalk on blue paper. 65.2598.

Nicolas Bernard Lépicié, France, 1735–1784.
Le jeune écolier. Pastel, ca. 1770.
65.2663.

Rosalba Carriera, Venice, 1675–1757.
60   *Louis XV as a Boy. Pastel. 65.2655.*

François Hubert Drouais, France, 1727–1775.
Mademoiselle Hainaut.
Oil on canvas, 1762. 65.2640.

Hubert Robert, France, 1733–1808.
62   L'Escalier des lavandières. Oil on canvas, 1796. 65.2653.

Jean-Baptiste Perronneau, France, 1715–1783.
The Earl of Huntingdon. Oil on canvas, ca. 1753. 65.2652.

Covered vase, one of a pair.
Meissen porcelain, Kakiemon decoration, ca. 1730.

64   *65.2032.*

Magot as flower holder with removable head and right hand.
Blanc-de-chine Chantilly porcelain, ormolu collar, ca. 1760.
65.1987.

One of a pair of magots. Meissen porcelain, ca. 1725. 65.2073.

Covered jar. Chantilly porcelain, Kakiemon decoration,
66   chased bronze-gilt mounts, ca. 1740–50. 65.1915.

Covered ewer and basin. Chantilly porcelain, Kakiemon decoration,
chased bronze-gilt mounts, ca. 1740–50. 65.1916.

Ewer. Decorator Xrowet. Vincennes porcelain,
gold mounts, 1753. 65.1816.

Tray. Decorator Levé père. "Rose Pompadour" Sèvres porcelain, 1757.
65.1784.

"Jardinière à éventail" (flower holder) and stand,
one of a garniture of three. Decorator Dodin.
70   *Sèvres porcelain, 1758. 65.1817.*

Pair of tulip stands.
Royal blue, apple green, apricot, and turquoise panels.
Sèvres porcelain, 1760. 65.1787–8.

Pair of cachepots. Decorator Thevenet père.
"Rose marbré" Sèvres porcelain, 1762.

72   *65.1814–5.*

Ecuelle and tray. Decorator Tandard.
Sèvres porcelain, 1763. 65.1906.

Ecuelle. Decorator Aloncle.
74 *Sèvres porcelain, 1764. 65.1873.*

Covered butter tub and dish. "Œil-de-Perdrix" royal blue Sèvres
porcelain, 1767. Twelve dinner plates and seven oval platters from this service are in the
collection. 65.1839.

Oval dish from the "Cameo Service" of Empress Catherine II of Russia,
consisting of 744 pieces. Decorated by Dodin, Niquet, Boulanger, Prevost.
76 *Bleu céleste and Pompeian red Sèvres porcelain, 1778. 1907.*

Pair of musician groups with children.
Model by Johann Peter Melchior. Frankenthal porcelain, ca. 1780.
65.2101–2.

Shepherdess playing lute.
78   *Derby porcelain, ca. 1750–54. 65.2189.*

Guitar player and drinking boy with attached flowering branches.
White Derby porcelain, ca. 1750–54. 65.2194–5.

Tureen with cover.
80   *Longton Hall porcelain, ca. 1750. 65.2175.*

Louis XV, perhaps after a marble bust by Jean-Baptiste Lemoyne,
made for Cardinal de Rohan of Strasbourg. White glazed Ludwigsburg
faience, 1746. 65.2014.

Jean-Louis Lemoyne (attributed), Paris, 1665–1755.
Posthumous portrait of François de Lamotte Fenélon.
Terra-cotta, 1724. 65.2213.

82

Jean-Baptiste Defernex, Paris, 1729–83.
Mademoiselle Dangeville. Terra-cotta,
signed and dated 1752. 65.2219.

Augustin Pajou, Paris, 1730–1809.
Madame Olivier. Terra-cotta,
84   *signed and dated 1774. 65.2218.*

Pygmaleon and Galatea, after Etienne-Maurice Falconet, Paris, 1716–91.
Decorator Louis-Antoine Le Grand. Biscuit group on royal
blue base, Sèvres porcelain, ca. 1790. 65.1812.

86

Baigneuse, after Christophe Gabriel Allegrain, Paris, 1710–95.
Marble, ca. 1780. 65.2206.

Claude Michel called Clodion, 1738–1814.
Two Bacchantes Dancing and Cupid.
Terra-cotta, signed and dated 1800. 65.2212.

Joseph-Charles Marin, Paris, 1759–1834.
Faunesse with Tambourine. Terra-cotta,
late 18th century. 65.2221.

Jean-Antoine Houdon, Paris, 1741–1828.
Charles-François Fontaine de Bire.
Marble, signed and dated 1786. 65.2203.

Joseph Chinard, Lyon, 1756–1813.
Madame M. Charpentier as a Painter.
90   *Original plaster, signed. 65.2208.*

Joseph Chinard, Lyon, 1756–1813.
Portrait bust of a man.
Terra-cotta, signed. 65.2216.

Pair of reading and writing putti, model of the factory of Dihl et Guerhard.
Biscuit porcelain, Paris, 1781. Used by Johann Peter Melchior at Frankenthal
for a memorial to Elector Karl Theodor of the Palatinate. 65.2097–8.

Nereid Riding a Sea Monster.
Bronze, Florence, ca. 1560.
94   *65.2228.*

Pair of Chenets (firedogs) with tritons blowing conch shells,
perhaps by Antoine Moureau after models by Lambert-Sigisbert Adam.
Ormolu, Paris, ca. 1750. 65.2252–3.

Pair of Chenets (firedogs) with cupid and girl and the arms of Poland.
Ormolu, Paris, ca. 1760. Probably made for Stanislaus I Leszczynski,
96   *King of Poland and Duke of Lorraine. 65.2250–1.*

Pair of coupled fish vases. Ch'ing dynasty porcelain, first half of the 18th century,
ormolu mounts in the manner of Jean-Claude Duplessis, Paris, ca. 1750. Perhaps
presented by Louis XV to Madame de Pompadour. 65.2260–1.

*Vase and cover. "Blue Mazarin" porcelain, Ch'ing dynasty,
1st half of 18th century. Ormolu mounts
in the manner of Pierre Germain, Paris, ca. 1750. 65.2262.*

98

Pendule en cartel (wall clock), case with cupids in ormolu,
manner of Charles Cressent, dial inscribed: Moisy, Paris, ca. 1745.
65.2231.

Paul Lamerie, London, working 1712–1751.
Fruit basket with the arms of the Duke of Montrose.
100   *Silver, 1744. 65.2307.*

Imported Chinese incised lacquer cabinet on Charles II gilt-wood stand.
London, late 17th century. 65.2528.

Commode, manner of Charles Cressent.
Veneered kingwood, inlaid with ebony and brass, ormolu mounts,
102   *Paris, ca. 1745. 65.2510.*

*One of a set of six fauteuils and canapé covered with Beauvais tapestry
depicting fables after designs by Jean-Baptiste Oudry.
Beechwood, Paris Louis XV period. 65.2495.*

Commode. Veneered kingwood inlaid with palisander wood,
104   *ormolu mounts, Louis XV period. 65.2509.*

Commode. Veneered black lacquer with Chinoiserie decoration,
ormolu mounts, Paris, ca. 1760. 65.2515.

106

Guéridon (table). Veneered kingwood and tulipwood
with marquetry decoration, ormolu mounts,
Louis XVI period. 65.2503.

Ecritoire, attributed to Jean-Henri Riesener.
Veneered harewood (mahogany), ormolu mounts,
Paris, ca. 1780. 65.2505.

Index

ARTISTS AND WORKS OF ART